malt whisky

discovering, exploring, enjoying

malt whisky

discovering, exploring, enjoying

ian wisniewski

photography by **alan williams**

RYLAND
PETERS
& SMALL

LONDON NEW YORK

First published in the United States in 2003
by Ryland Peters & Small, Inc
519 Broadway
5th Floor
New York NY 10012
www.rylandpeters.com

10 9 8 7 6 5 4 3 2 1

Printed and bound in China

Designer Luis Peral-Aranda
Editor Miriam Hyslop
Location Research Claire Hector
Picture Research Emily Westlake
Production Louise Bartrum
Art Director Gabriella Le Grazie
Publishing Director Alison Starling

Library of Congress Cataloging-in-Publication Data

Wisniewski, Ian.
  Malt whisky : discovering, exploring, enjoying / Ian
Wisniewski.
    p. cm.
  ISBN 1-84172-504-8
  1. Whiskey--Scotland. I. Title.
  TP605.W56 2003
  641.2'52'09411--dc21
                                    2003008797

contents

As one of the world's most historic spirits, malt whisky is also one of the most progressive and innovative. A growing range of malts, including vintages, special finishes and longer-aged styles, continues to enthral ever more devotees. Revered throughout Europe, Asia, and North and South America, the future has never looked better.

where it's at

modern classic

Thriving on cult status around the world, malt whisky attracts a more knowledgeable and devoted following than any other spirit. Even more extraordinary is how recently this has happened, essentially since the 1980s.

Malt whisky (distilled from barley) was the original style of whisky produced in Scotland. However, when blended whisky (malt blended with grain whiskies) was developed in the mid-19th century, this lighter style soon became more popular.

The small number of malts that continued to be available in Scotland were only sold by specialized retailers, and bought by the gentry, for whom malt was the "authentic" style of Scotch whisky. Malts continued their elite existence until the 1960s, when a lone pioneer, The Glenfiddich, became more widely available.

At that time sales of blended whisky were growing, prompting distilleries to modernize and increase production capacity. However, despite forecasts of continued growth, sales of blends began to decrease during the late 1970s.

With less malts required for blends, and the price of whisky slumping, many distilleries switched to part-time production or even closed. As storing whisky is an expensive undertaking, there had to be another way of increasing sales.

Consequently, the number of malts began to grow beyond what had become an established trio of The Glenfiddich, Glenmorangie, and The Glenlivet, supplemented by independent bottlers such as Gordon & MacPhail and William Cadenhead.

While the mass market remained oblivious to the difference between malts and blends, connoisseurs were developing a special relationship with malts. This encouraged more contenders and a wider range of styles onto the ˙ market, including longer-aged malts.

THE EARLIEST RECORDED REFERENCE TO MALT WHISKY DATES FROM 1494

As appreciation of malt whisky continued to evolve, a changing price structure also brought malts within reach of a larger audience. During the 1970s the least expensive, or "entry-level," malts were typically twice the price of equivalent quality blends. By the 1990s there was little to choose between them.

Although this had the potential to devalue some of the aspirational qualities of malt whisky, continued specialization means that there are always more levels for the whisky lover to ascend. Longer maturation periods, as

AS A SINGLE MALT HAILS FROM A SPECIFIC DISTILLERY WITH AN INDIVIDUAL PROVENANCE, THERE IS AN IMMEDIATE TALKING POINT, AS WITH FINE WINE FROM A CHATEAU

well as cask strength, special finishes, vintages, single barrel, and other limited-edition styles (see page 42) maintain that vital sense of aspiration.

The range continued to grow with the launch of The Classic Malts in 1987. United Distillers, owning a vast number of malt distilleries and blended Scotch brands, compiled a set of six malts marketed under the collective term "Classic Malts."

Each malt exemplifies the characteristics of the region in which it is produced, Glenkinchie (from the Lowlands), Talisker, Dalwhinnie and Oban (the Highlands), Cragganmore (Speyside), and Lagavulin (Islay). This line-up provides a malt whisky tour of Scotland that can be experienced by the glass.

United Distillers (now part of Diageo) followed the success of The Classic Malts with another service catering to the fan club, entitled The Rare Malts. Launched in 1995, this is an annual release of up to five rare malts, including those from "silent" distilleries which are no longer in production, and so highly desirable.

WITH SUCH A WIDE RANGE
OF MALTS PRODUCED,
RANGING FROM ELEGANT
AND FRUITY, TO RICHER,
SMOKIER STYLES
THERE REALLY IS A MALT
TO SUIT EVERY PALATE

The traditional theory, that our palates graduate from blended to malt whisky, and correspondingly from elegant, fruity malts to more challenging, peaty styles, is now becoming outdated. As consumer taste is continually evolving, demonstrated by a move from white wines to the greater complexity of reds, blended whiskies are increasingly bypassed as more drinkers reach straight for a malt.

Like every spirit, malts should be judged on what they offer rather than on preconceptions, particularly as many flavors that make wine so popular also appear in malts. Vanilla, chocolate, fresh and cooked fruit, as well as herbs and spices, are a few examples. Together with peaty, smoky notes, delivered with varying degrees of intensity, there really is a malt to suit every palate.

With access to ever-more books, websites, chat rooms, and malt whisky societies, it's easy for beginners as well as connoisseurs to develop their level of knowledge and commitment to malts. Numerous distilleries also welcome visitors and offer membership of their own "friends of" societies which continues to broaden malt's appeal.

Phenomenal growth has seen malt whisky sales rise from 12.6 million bottles in 1980 to 57 million bottles in 2002, with around 90 malt whisky distilleries currently operational.

How much more popular and specialized malts become remains to be seen, though how much members of the malt clan are prepared to pay for what they love is perfectly clear. The current world record price for a bottle of malt is £25,877.50 ($41,417.20).

The character of a malt whisky stems from its ingredients—barley, water, and yeast—together with the influences that enhance the original aromas and flavors during the production process. This includes malting, peating, fermentation, and distillation, before aging in oak casks in Scotland for a minimum of three years.

how it's made

ALTHOUGH BARLEY
IS A PRINCIPAL
INGREDIENT, IT IS
CONSIDERED A
MINOR INFLUENCE
ON THE CHARACTER
OF WHISKY,
ESSENTIALLY
CONTRIBUTING
MALTY, BISCUITY
FLAVORS

barley and water

The method of producing malt whisky, using barley, water, and yeast, originally developed on a basis of trial and error. Even with continual advances in research and technology, it remains difficult to quantify the exact influence of each stage of the production process. The only certainty is that changing any part of the process can alter the character of the resulting spirit.

Distilling spirits has always been a case of using the local harvest. Spring barley, the standard choice among distillers in Scotland, is sown in March to early April, and harvested in August to September.

There are a number of varieties of spring barley to choose from. Current favorites include Optic, Chalice, and Decanter, all high-performance varieties developed during the 1990s.

However, a consensus among distillers is that the barley variety doesn't make any difference to the resulting flavor of a malt whisky.

Much of the credit for a malt's individual character has traditionally gone to the distillery's water source. Needless to say, the influence of water is a far easier concept to understand, compared to the technicalities of the production process, such as a copper-pot still.

Distilleries draw on a variety of water sources, rivers, streams, springs, and lochs, which yield water with a varying range of characteristics.

But the degree to which these characteristics actually determine the final flavor of a particular malt whisky is difficult or even impossible, to quantify.

The minerals that give water flavor, for example, cannot pass through the distillation system, and using demineralized ("neutral") water is standard practice when bottling malts (see page 37).

While water is an important factor, it is far less influential than the effect of distillation and aging, which together account for the majority of the resulting flavor.

malting and peating

Barley's essential asset is the starch that it contains. For the grain, starch serves as a food source, enabling it to start developing roots and a shoot. For the distiller, the level of starch within the barley determines the yield of alcohol. It's a simple formula: the more starch, the greater the yield.

The grain's starch content is initially enclosed within cell walls. A process known as malting is used to break down these cell walls and release the starch.

The first stage of malting involves "steeping" (soaking) the grains in water to hydrate them, and then transferring the barley from steeping tanks to allow it to germinate.

The more high-tech approach uses special germination vessels, with computers providing the most appropriate temperature. The more traditional hands-on method is to spread the barley across a malting floor, and control the temperature by "turning" the grains (moving them around) using either a spade or a rake known as a "plough."

As the grain starts to grow during germination, it breaks down the cell walls in order to access the starch, while also beginning to secrete diastase (a group of enzymes).

At this point, before the grain begins to use up any starch, further growth is prevented by "kilning" (drying) the grain, using hot air.

If the barley is to be "peated," then peat is also added to the kiln. This creates peat smoke that is conducted to the grain, and essentially absorbed by the grain's husk.

Peating contributes a range of peaty, smoky aromas and flavors, with the level of peating depending on the style of malt being produced. For a lightly peated malt, small amounts of peat are added to the kiln. Medium and heavily peated malts require correspondingly larger amounts of peat, which are added to the kiln at regular intervals over a longer period.

Only a few distilleries, including the Balvenie, Bowmore, Highland Park, Laphroaig, and Springbank, continue to malt their own barley. The majority are supplied by commercial maltsters, which operate on a large scale, and also peat the barley (as appropriate) according to each distillery's individual requirements.

mashing, fermenting, distilling

Once malted, the barley is "milled" (crushed) to prepare it for the next stage of the production process, "mashing." The barley is mixed with hot water, in large vessels called "mash tuns." Contact with hot water activates the conversion of the starches into sugars.

The resulting sugary liquid, known as "wort," is drained from the mash tuns and transferred into "washbacks" (fermentation vessels). Yeast is added to the wort to start fermentation, converting the sugars into alcohol. The result is a liquid known as "wash," with a strength of around 8–10% alcohol by volume (abv).

The wash is subsequently distilled twice in a pot still, which is the most historic method of distillation. Heating the wash causes the alcohol to vaporize, and the vapors rise up the neck of the still, which extends from the bulbous base. The neck conducts vapors to the

THE SIZE AND SHAPE OF A COPPER STILL HAS A SIGNIFICANT INFLUENCE ON THE CHARACTER OF THE SPIRIT

condenser, where a cooler temperature causes them to condense, and this liquid is collected as alcohol.

Separate stills are used for each distillation, a wash still for the first, and a spirit still for the second. The wash still produces "low wines," with an alcoholic strength of around 25% abv. The low wines are enhanced by the spirit still, which raises the alcoholic strength of what is known as "new-make" spirit to around 70% abv.

Stills are fashioned from copper, which is a supreme conductor of heat. Being a highly malleable metal is another asset, as the shapes and sizes of pot stills vary widely among distilleries, from short and bulbous to slimmer and taller.

Lighter, fruitier flavors are fostered by a narrower still with a longer neck, while a more bulbous still with a shorter neck generates richer flavors. This is because the boiling point of heavier flavor compounds is higher than lighter compounds, and as they rise up a tall neck, the temperature cools. As this causes them to condense, they return to the base of the still. A still with a short neck has a less variable temperature, and richer flavor compounds continue through to the condenser.

THE RELATIONSHIP BETWEEN THE MATURING SPIRIT AND THE OAK CASK IS SO COMPLEX THAT IT IS STILL NOT FULLY UNDERSTOOD. THE INTERACTION OF THE TWO IS VITAL AS IT DEVELOPS FLAVORS NOT PRESENT IN THE NEW-MAKE SPIRIT

aging in oak casks

Each distillery's new-make spirit has an individual flavor profile—from light- to fuller-bodied. This is known as the "distillery character." The object of aging the spirit in oak casks is to reach a balance between its "distillery" and "maturation character" (flavors resulting from the aging process).

A malt's flavor profile continually evolves as it matures in a cask. The aging potential of each malt varies, and they reach different stages of maturity in their own time. An oak cask influences a lighter malt far more readily than a fuller-bodied malt, for example, particularly if it has been peated. Similarly, longer aging sees the cask exert a greater influence, imparting distinctive "oakyness." That's why an older malt is not automatically superior to a younger one. Each is a different expression with its own appeal.

The choice of barrels is another significant element of the aging process, as each type of cask contributes a different range of flavors. New, unused oak casks would easily overwhelm a malt. That's why the standard choice is casks that have already been used to age either bourbon or sherry, and so are already "seasoned."

Sherry casks impart rich, dry sweetness with fruit flavors such as apricots, figs, raisins, a range of spices including ginger, nutmeg, and cloves, and indulgent favorites such as walnuts and chocolate. A higher level of tannin, compared to bourbon barrels, also promotes greater body and structure. Bourbon barrels yield abundant vanilla, and related flavors such as fudge, toffee, butterscotch, and crème brûlée. A range of ripe summer fruits, like melons and raspberries, together with honey, sherbert, coconut, and almonds are also part of the package.

The relationship between the maturing spirit and the oak cask is so complex that it is still not fully understood. The interaction of the two is a vital factor, because it creates an additional range of flavors, which are not present in either the oak cask or the new-make spirit.

Malt whisky is produced in the Lowlands, Highlands, Campbeltown, and the island of Islay in Scotland. Whisky from each region has specific characteristics. Intense Islay malts reveal abundant peat, smoke, and marine influences, for example, while the classic range of Highland characteristics include fresh fruit together with floral, heather, and honeyed notes.

where it's made

THE 10-YEAR-OLD TALISKER, DISTILLED ON THE
ISLE OF SKYE, DELIVERS DRIED FRUIT FLAVORS
AND A WAFT OF SMOKE BALANCED BY SALTY
LEMON AND DARK CHOCOLATE, WHILE A FRESH
BURST OF SMOKY MALT ADDS A MEMORABLE FINISH

the highlands

As the largest geographical region, with the greatest number of distilleries, the Highlands extends north of the Lowlands, incorporating Speyside and several islands such as Orkney, Skye, Mull, and Jura. Consequently, the Highlands offers the most comprehensive range of styles, which also makes it the most difficult region to define.

Classic Highland characteristics include fresh and dried fruit, particularly apples, pears and citrus, together with floral, heather, and honeyed notes. While some distilleries produce unpeated malts, others span a variety of peating levels, ranging from gentle hints of smoke to a rich pungency. Talisker 10 year old for example, delivers dried fruit flavors and a waft of smoke balanced by salty lemon and dark chocolate, while a fresh burst of smoky malt adds a memorable finish.

Although technically part of the Highlands, Speyside malts have a separate identity, with a sophistication that combines balance and complexity. Around half of all Scotland's malt whisky distilleries are actually located in this area, with the largest concentration of distilleries in Dufftown. This accounts for the local rhyme, "Rome was built on seven hills, but Dufftown's built on seven stills." Unlike the rhyme, this total has continually been revised, and the town is now host to six operational distilleries: The Balvenie, Dufftown, The Glenfiddich, Glendullan, Kininvie, and Mortlach.

the lowlands

Renowned as the most delicate style, Lowland malts thrive on floral, grassy aromas and sweet fruit flavors balanced by a citrus freshness that concludes with a dry finish. These characteristics make Lowland malts an ideal introduction to malt whisky, though Lowland malts also offer individuality.

The number of distilleries in this region has declined from a 19th-century peak of around 35 to three, Bladnoch, Glenkinchie, and Auchentoshan. (Although malts from "silent" distilleries, such as Ladyburn and Rosebank, are still available).

The simplest way to explore the Lowlands style is to compare the region's most readily available malts, Glenkinchie and Auchentoshan. Glenkinchie's

WHILE MALTS CAN CERTAINLY DELIVER A CLASSIC RANGE OF REGIONAL CHARACTERISTICS, THEY ALSO OFFER PLENTY OF INDIVIDUALITY

proximity to Scotland's capital accounts for it's also being known as "the Edinburgh malt." The Glenkinchie 10 year old, which is lightly peated, displays Lowland grassiness and a waft of smoke on the nose. The palate reveals fresh, ripe fruit, with subtle oak notes and malt, with a dry, spicy, smoky finish. Auchentoshan's location, adjacent to Scotland's "other capital city," lends it the name "Glasgow's malt." The Auchentoshan 10 year old also shows the classic regional characteristics of light, dried grass aromas, with linseed oil and crème brûlée. The palate's creamy lusciousness balances biscuity dryness with underlying gingerbread and citrus.

islay and campbeltown

The earliest malts may have been distilled on Islay. An abundance of peat bogs and water sources make Islay a natural habitat for distilleries. The only obstacle to self-sufficiency is a climate hostile to barley. However, the frequent winter gales and no lack of rain in any season actually belie a temperate climate throughout the year, which is ideal for maturing malt whisky.

With seven working distilleries, Islay malts are renowned as the most intense, delivering abundant peat, smoke, and marine influences. This definition is certainly fulfilled by Ardbeg, Laphroaig, and Lagavulin, though each also provides a full supporting cast of other flavors. Meanwhile, Bruichladdich, Bunnahabhain, and Caol Ila offer classic Islay characteristics in a mellower form, with Bowmore poised midway between both ends of the scale.

Even different ages of the same malt offer varying degrees of intensity. Laphroaig, which includes a subtitle on the bottle label: "The most richly flavoured of all Scotch whiskies," is a prime example. The 10-year-old Laphroaig delivers pungent, peaty, smoky aromas garnished with brine in the initial flourish. A range of vanilla pod and nutty fruitcake aromas subsequently open up, with the smoke reduced to an underlying waft.

As the influence of peat mellows the longer a whisky matures, the Laphroaig 15 year old has milder smoke and lightly toasty aromas, supported by a hint of freshly mown hay, sea air, citrus, and vanilla.

An even more mature specimen, The 1960 Vintage, is wonderfully enigmatic. Aromas resemble a breath of sea air, accompanied by wafts of smoky lemon, vanilla pod, and chargrilled toastyness. The elegant, mellow palate unfolds with smoky vanilla, nutty fruitcake, smoky lemon, apples baked with cloves, orange ripeness, and a burst of creamy malt, balanced by a salty lemon garnish. It's a perfect way to experience Islay's distinctive style.

Campbeltown, on the Kintyre peninsula, is a small town that was once the center of Scotland's malt whisky industry, with a total of 34 distilleries established there between 1820–1930. Its sheltered harbor made this an ideal transit point for shipping malts to Glasgow, and then on to other countries around the world. Another advantage is a mild climate (modified by the Gulf Stream) which is ideal for maturing malt whisky. Campbeltown soon established a superior reputation for pungent malts, with distinctive smoky, sea spray characteristics.

The grand total of distilleries has dwindled, and former distillery buildings can be seen around the town. Ben Mhor, for example, is part of the bus station, and the Campbeltown Creamery was originally the Burnside distillery.

Only Springbank and Glen Scotia remained operational distilleries. Dating from 1832, Glen Scotia produces

a 14-year-old single malt, while Springbank's extensive repertoire has a devoted following.

Still owned by the Mitchell family, which established the distillery in 1828, Springbank is a rarity in undertaking each step of the production process, including malting, on the premises. The distillery is actually the source of three different styles of malt whisky, each produced using varying distillation regimes and peating levels.

Hazleburn is unpeated, while the eponymous Springbank is lightly peated, and accounts for the majority of production, whereas Longrow is heavily peated.

The Longrow 1989, 13 year old is an ideal ambassador for the distillery's craftsmanship. An ultra-delicate palate opens with toffee and fudge, dark chocolate, plums and damsons, vanilla and a waft of peaty, oaky notes, garnished with citrus. As though that weren't enough, the finish combines vanilla, chocolate, raisins, and orange.

The Mitchell family is also regenerating Campbeltown's legacy, re-opening the Glengyle distillery in 2004. Established in 1872, Glengyle had been silent since 1925. This actually marks a return of ownership, as the Mitchell family established the distillery before selling it in 1919 to a local consortium, West Highland Malt Distilleries, which also owned other distilleries in Campbeltown.

THE BAILIE NICOL

→ BLEND OF ←

→ Old Scotch Wh

PRODUCE OF
SCOTLAND

As one of the most innovative spirit categories, malt whisky has developed a dynamic portfolio of styles. Most are continually available, while limited-edition releases have become another growing sector. The choice includes single and vatted malts, longer-matured, cask strength, special finishes, vintages, and single-barrel styles, together with commemorative bottlings marking various events and anniversaries.

malt whisky styles

single and vatted malt

A single malt is bottled exclusively from the malt whisky produced by a single distillery, which it is named after. While some styles of malt are only aged in sherry casks, and others only in bourbon barrels, most distilleries produce single malts matured in both types of casks.

As each type of cask contributes different flavors, the character of a malt can be created by varying the proportions. The initial flavors of the Bruichladdich 15 year old, for example, stem from bourbon barrels, with a medley of vanilla, crème brûlée, coconut, fruit trifle, and a dusting of cocoa powder. The influence of the sherry cask subsequently emerges, adding gingerbread, butterscotch, and oaky notes to the ensemble.

Vatted malts are a "vatting" (blend) of malt whiskies distilled by more than one distillery. This term stems from the "vat" (vessel) in which blending takes place. By combining single malts that harmonize and complement each other, the resulting complexity exceeds the individual merits of each malt. A vatted malt may combine 10 or more individual malts, with an extraordinary total being the 100 single malts in Chivas Brothers Century of Malts.

The age statement that appears on a bottle label, such as 10 or 15 year old, refers to the age of the youngest malt used. A recipe may also include older malts, depending on the house style, or to maintain a consistent flavor.

The typical, and minimum, bottling strength is 40% abv (the alcoholic strength reduces as a malt matures, and is finally adjusted by adding water to reach the appropriate strength). However, malts are also bottled at higher strengths, such as 43% or 45% abv. As the flavor profile of a malt changes according to the alcoholic strength, this is a relevant factor.

A malt labeled "cask strength" is bottled at the alcoholic strength it reaches in the cask, when judged mature by the master distiller. Cask strength malts are prized for showing the most "natural" character. A'bunadh for example is bottled in batches, with the cask strength around 59%–61% abv, so the flavor can vary slightly. But this element of individuality is exactly what the devotees desire.

special finishes

As a subsequent aging period applied to mature malt whisky, a "special finish" uses a specific type of cask to provide additional flavors. Inaugurated by Glenmorangie in 1994, this approach actually continues a traditional practice, and is a case of a practicality being elevated into a speciality.

During the late 19th and early 20th century, fortified wines, including madeira, port, and sherry, were shipped to Scotland in casks and bottled locally. This meant numerous empty casks that could be "recycled" and filled with malt whisky, ready to be shipped to British colonies throughout the Empire. As several months could easily elapse between a cask being filled and arriving at its long-haul destination, the cask had a discernible influence on the flavor of the whisky.

Glenmorangie's first special finish used port casks to finish a malt matured in bourbon barrels. Madeira, sherry, and malaga cask finishes followed. Some distilleries have since used a range of wine and spirit casks for special finishes, typically lasting 6 months to 2 years, with Cuban rum casks, for example, behind The Glenfiddich Havana Reserve 21 year old.

An irresistible line-up of limited-edition special finishes are also produced. These include Glenmorangie's Côte de Beaune finish, using wine casks from Burgundy, while the Balvenie Islay Cask 17 year old was finished in casks previously containing an Islay malt. This added a waft of Islay peat, which balances The Balvenie's vanilla, honeyed, subtle sweetness.

Glenmorangie's 1981 Sauternes Wood Finish featured 20-year-old malt finished in casks that previously held the most celebrated premier "grand cru" dessert wine from Bordeaux's Sauternes region. And the result? A luscious palate delivers honeyed, vanilla, fresh apple, and *tarte tatin* notes, together with lemon meringue creamyness. Sensational.

MALT WHISKY

SINGLE CASK SCOTCH MALT WHISKY

DATE DISTILLED	Dec 71
DATE BOTTLED	Oct 01
AGED IN OAK	29 yrs
PROOF STRENGTH	96.6° 55.2% vol
CONTENTS BY VOL	70 cl

vintage malts

Birthdays, anniversaries, and special events create a natural demand for malts bearing a vintage date, helping to make sure every year can be a good one for malt whisky distilleries. Only exceptional malts are released as a vintage, and as malt whisky is distilled to be consistent, it is the choice of cask and aging process that provides the annual variations.

While the vintage date confirms the year a malt was distilled, the bottling date is equally important, indicating how long it has been aged.

As vintages are limited editions, the master distiller is able to choose exceptional casks that show the distillery character in a far more individual manner. However, vintage variations can also be attributed to other elements of the production process. Numerous distilleries have varied their peating levels, for example, which has a significant influence on the resulting flavor. The Macallan is now very lightly peated, though the level was significantly higher from the mid-1930s to '50s. Bruichladdich also changed from a heavily peated malt to a much lighter style in 1960.

A fascinating innovation is The Macallan's Replica Series. This limited-edition series "recreates" the flavor of historic vintages by vatting more recently distilled malts. The inaugural 1874 Replica was launched in 1996, followed by the 1861 Replica in 2001, and the 1841 Replica in 2002. This provides a rare opportunity to experience an "antique" vintage taste, particularly as Replicas are presented in a facsimile of the original bottle.

single barrel and other limited-edition styles

While many styles of malt are bottled from a vatting (blend) of casks to achieve a consistent flavor, the appeal of a single barrel malt is its individuality. This stems from the fact that even the same types of barrels filled with the same batch of spirit, and aged for the same period next to each other in the same warehouse, will never have an identikit influence. The resulting malts always show some differences. These may be minor, but they can also be major. Consequently, a single barrel malt gives master distillers the chance to select individual casks that are an outstanding expression of the house style.

A 28-year-old Talisker released in 2002 was limited to 100 bottles filled from a single cask

A traditional limited-edition style, known as The Manager's Dram, can also be bottled from a single cask selected by distillery managers, and sold or presented to distillery employees. The rarity of these bottlings, which only come onto the market as and when employees decide to part with them, guarantees that they are highly sought.

Major events are also a natural prompt for limited-editions. Highland Park on Orkney, for example, released 2,000 bottles of a special 12 year old at cask strength to elevate the Millennium celebrations.

Similarly, the Queen's Golden Jubilee in 2002 was marked by Bowmore which produced 648 bottles of the "Queen's Cask." This cask was filled in August 1980, when Her Majesty Queen Elizabeth II visited Bowmore on Islay.

While malts are almost always aged in either bourbon or sherry barrels, limited-edition bottlings can also offer alternatives. Glenfarclas released a 21-year-old malt, distilled in 1979, that was matured entirely in a port pipe (cask). Similarly, Glenmorangie Cognac Matured was an edition of 850 bottles of Glenmorangie matured for 14 years in casks that previously aged cognac.

longer maturation

While a wider choice of more mature malts is increasingly available, as distilleries extend their portfolios with longer-aged styles, they appear in strictly limited numbers because stocks are inevitably rare. One reason is that during the 1960s and '70s, the typical age limit for malts was considered to be 10–15 years. Finding casks of older malts can therefore be a matter of serendipity as much as strategy, though laying down casks for longer maturation is now more established.

Different malts and individual casks offer various aging potential. As the influence of the cask increases the longer a malt is aged, it can become overwhelming, resulting in a lifeless "woody" flavor that no one would want to drink. The aim is to reach an impressive age while retaining a balanced flavor.

Also, as evaporation from the cask means losing around 2% in volume annually, with alcoholic strength also declining, a significant amount of malt is sacrificed during longer aging.

Bowmore, The Balvenie, The Glenfiddich, The Glenlivet, and The Macallan are among those releasing 40- and 50-year-old malts. The Macallan and Gordon & MacPhail have even released 60 year olds, while The Dalmore filled 12 bottles of a 62 year old in 2002.

The price of an older malt, with $9,500–$16,000 a bottle not unusual, does of course reflect rarity value and the expense of longer aging, not to mention the master distiller's skill. And then there is the question of the resulting flavor. Exactly how amazing it is depends entirely on your own palate. Similarly, whether paying such high prices and then actually drinking the malt is a dream come true is entirely up to you, and your budget.

INDEPENDENT BOTTLERS HAVE STARTED TO DIVERSIFY AND BUY THEIR OWN DISTILLERIES, WHICH SAW BRUICHLADDICH AND BENROMACH COME BACK INTO PRODUCTION

independent bottlers

In addition to distilleries releasing their own malt whiskies, known as "proprietary" brands, independent bottlers also release single malts, buying casks either from whisky brokers or directly from distilleries. These are bottled under the company's own label, while also stipulating the distillery which produced the malt.

Independent bottlers actually continue a 19th-century tradition, when distilleries sold casks of malt whisky to grocers, as well as to wine and spirit merchants. Customers brought their own bottles to the shop, which were filled directly from a cask.

Thriving on the accolade of being Scotland's oldest independent bottler, William Cadenhead was established in Aberdeen in 1842 as a wine and spirit merchant. It remained in family ownership until the company was acquired in the early 1970s by the Mitchell family, proprietors of Springbank distillery in Campbeltown.

Founded in 1895, Gordon & MacPhail's range of Connoisseurs Choice exceeds 40 single malts and includes highly desirable rarities, together with limited-edition commemorative bottlings. In 1993 the company entered a new era, by acquiring Benromach distillery in Speyside, which had been silent since 1983. Other independent bottlers followed suit. Murray McDavid, who's Mission range comprises rare whiskies from various distilleries, acquired the Bruichladdich distillery on Islay in 2001, which had been silent since 1994.

blended whisky

The concept of blending malt and grain whisky developed during the 1860s. At that time malt whiskies were considered too intense and smoky, and quality was also variable. Blending malts with lighter grain whiskies (distilled from malted barley together with wheat or corn) yielded a mellower style of whisky, while also providing a more consistent flavor. Being a "new" style, fashionability must also have boosted the popularity of blends, which really took off in the late 19th century.

Although lighter than malts, grain whiskies nevertheless offer an individual flavor profile that reflects the distillery's "house style," which develops through a minimum of three years aging in oak casks. However, the real value of grain whiskies is the interaction they have with malts in attaining balance and complexity, as a blend typically comprises up to 40 or more malt and grain whiskies.

Having created a blend, the challenge is to maintain a consistent flavor. As the availability of certain whiskies can

vary, knowing which whiskies to use as "replacements" is a considerable skill.

Chief blenders buy malt and grain whiskies from other distilleries, and although it's a competitive business, rivals trade with each other perfectly happily.

The ratio of malts to grain in a recipe depends on the style being produced, though 12-year-old and older blends tend to contain a higher percentage of malts. This doesn't automatically guarantee a finer blend, since it is the character of the malts used, whether lighter or richer, and the balance they attain, which is significant.

There is also an element of "alchemy" involved in blending. Even combining one malt with one grain whisky creates an interaction between them, which in turn produces flavors that are not present in either whisky individually. Which elements, and how many of the resulting flavors, are created by this action is impossible to rationalize.

While there's no need to have any prior knowledge or experience to enjoy malt whisky, knowing what to look for and how to assess a malt can certainly enhance the pleasure. Learning how to "nose" and taste a malt only entails a few practical guidelines, and the more you do it, the easier it becomes.

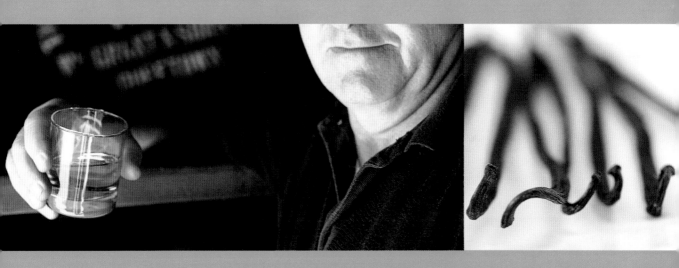

enjoying malt whisky

colors and glasses

The color of a malt may seem to indicate how it will taste, and give a sense of how long it has been aged, but color can be misleading. A number of older whiskies do have a darker color and richer flavor, but a lighter color doesn't automatically

THE COLOR IN MALT WHISKY DEVELOPS THROUGH AGING, AND IT IS DERIVED FROM THE CASK, AS NEW-MAKE SPIRIT IS COLORLESS WHEN DISTILLED

indicate a lighter style or younger malt. Even a 25 year old, for example, can have a golden amber color.

This is because the color of a malt also reflects the type of cask in which it was matured, and not just the length of aging. Malts aged in bourbon barrels have a lighter color, which can range from translucent pale yellow and gold to orange amber. This compares to a much darker range of color, from light amber through to reddish brown and mahogany, imparted by sherry casks.

An engraved glass is a traditional choice for serving malts, this decorative element making it seem more suitable for an indulgent occasion. However, a plain glass is actually better for assessing the color of a malt, since engraved glass tends to refract light into the malt.

A host of whisky glasses, in a range of shapes and sizes, have been specially designed by different producers. As the dimensions of a glass influence the way in which aromas and flavors are channeled and perceived, the same malt can taste slightly, or even significantly different, depending on the glass.

The style of glass used by professionals, a "tulip-shaped" bowl on a stem, is typically considered to direct the flavors and aromas in the best way. Another classic choice, the tumbler, has a much broader surface area, so the aromas are less channeled, and can be a little more difficult to gauge.

Malt whiskies are rarely served from a decanter, because seeing the original bottle is considered an essential part of the experience for many malt drinkers. However, some malts are sold in special decanters rather than bottles, which conveniently covers both options.

aromas

"Nosing" a whisky (inhaling the aromas) acts as an overture to tasting. Nosing is the method used by professionals to evaluate and compare whiskies. In fact, master distillers and chief blenders rarely taste samples. Having to assess 20 or more samples in a typical session explains why!

The "nose" (aroma) of a malt can initially be judged on whether it is "open" and the aromas accessible, or closed, which may also indicate that more patience is required for it to open up.

Aromas can be "released" by adding water and gently swirling the drink in a glass. However, since this also releases alcohol, the aim is to draw the aromas into the nose while avoiding the initial hit of alcohol (which attacks the olfactory sense).

The usual precaution is to allow the malt a moment to "settle" after swirling, then gently inhale the aromas, holding the glass a few inches below the nose. Pause for a moment, and as long as you detect aromas rather than alcohol, lower your nose a little deeper into the glass and inhale again.

Identifying the range of characteristics is inevitably a personal definition and whatever aromas you find are right for your nose. As adding water releases a "rush" of aromas, first impressions of a malt are inevitably the right ones.

The aromas may be integrated in a "package," or a sequence of notes that can be described individually, and as specifically as you like. Vanilla, for example, is an archetypal characteristic that

INHALING THE AROMAS OF MALT WHISKY IS AN INITIAL WAY TO JUDGE AND ENJOY IT. "NOSING" GIVES A GOOD IDEA OF THE FLAVORS YOU CAN EXPECT, BUT THERE ARE INEVITABLY SOME SURPRISES IN STORE WHEN YOU COME TO TASTE THE MALT

can be manifested in various forms, such as a vanilla pod, vanilla custard, or vanilla crème anglaise.

The nose continues to evolve as the malt "breathes," and the initial range of aromas will subsequently vary. The more complex a malt, the greater the range of aromas it will reveal, as long as you are patient (and haven't drunk it in the meantime).

Another technique used by professionals is the "palm method". Pouring a small amount of malt into the cupped palm of one hand, then rubbing both hands together to warm the malt, releases the aromas. These can be assessed by taking a series of quick inhalations from your cupped hands.

tasting

Malt whiskies range from light, refreshing, and elegantly fruity, to richer and more complex. Moving a malt around the palate (mouth), while taking in a little air, not only helps to reveal the full spectrum of flavors but also the texture (mouthfeel) which may be light and elegant, creamy, or rich and luscious.

Whether to add water when tasting whisky is up to you. The professional preference is to reduce the strength of the malt from 40% abv (alcohol by volume) to around 20% abv, by adding an equal amount of still spring water.

Lowering the alcoholic strength helps to reveal the flavor profile more readily. However, the alcoholic strength also determines the range of flavors. This explains why a malt tastes different at 40% abv compared from 20% abv.

Adding water is essential with a cask strength whisky, particularly if it's over 43% abv. The sheer intensity of the alcohol can make it difficult to discern, let alone enjoy, the flavor profile.

Progressively less water should be added to older malts. With a 10 year old, it's usual to add about half the amount of water compared to the amount of malt, and about a third when tasting a 15 year old. A few drops will "open up" a 21 year old, while a senior malt, such as a 50 year old, generally doesn't need any water.

Older whiskies also require more time to open up and reveal their full credentials. A useful tip is to pour your malt and then allow "one minute for every year" of age before you taste it.

You may not wish to wait that long, but a malt certainly evolves as it opens up, and tasting at subsequent intervals means the flavor you start with can vary from the one you end up with.

flavors

Primary tastes are detected by different parts of the tongue. Sweetness is picked up at the front, salty and sour notes midway, while bitterness is detected at the back of the tongue. But however much credit we give our palates, it is the olfactory sense that accounts for a large percentage of perceived taste.

How flavors are revealed is an initial consideration, with some showing as primary characteristics, while others play a more subtle supporting role, or serve as a garnish.

If the malt shows fruit, is this fresh, cooked, or dried fruit? Apples, for example, may appear as ripe, sweet red, or crisp, lightly tart green apples, or baked with hints of clove and honey. Similarly, citrus notes can show as fresh or dried zest, orange marmalade, lemon curd, lemon meringue, or salted lemon. A typical range of dried fruit includes raisins, figs, prunes, and apricots, while almonds and walnuts are also staples in malt whisky.

Malty, cereal, biscuity notes stem from the barley, while peating the barley adds a range of nuances. This results in various degrees of sweet and tart, earthy peatyness, and smokyness, ranging from wafts and embers to charred, bonfire notes.

Whatever the flavor profile, the essential question is whether the palate is balanced, harmonious, and of course rewarding. Another part of the experience is identifying different influences. This includes flavors from the casks and peating, as well as the effect of sea air on island malts (sea air permeates the cask during aging, adding salty, lemon notes).

The Bruichladdich 1986 Valinch from Islay is an ideal opportunity to test your palate. The initial flavors serve up various indulgences: butterscotch, fruitcake, and gingerbread, garnished with toasty, lemon, sea-salt notes. The palate becomes increasingly luscious with raisins and muscovado sweetness, culminating in roasted almonds delivered in a sustained, uninhibited manner. A triumph.

Beyond assessing a malt's texture, balance, and flavor delivery, another important element is the aftertaste, or "finish," and what the malt continues to deliver after swallowing. The finish can be short or sustained, and in that time may conjure up some entirely new flavors. Then again, the finish may serve up some, or even all of the flavors that appeared on the palate, and provide a lingering reminder of why you should have another sip.

collecting

As there are more ways to enjoy malt whisky than drinking it, collecting is another part of the appeal. Miniatures are the first step for many collectors, before graduating to full-sized bottles. An obvious advantage is that miniatures are far less expensive and use far less storage space.

Collectors are typically decried on the basis that malt whisky should be savoured, rather than exhibited in a cabinet. Many collectors agree, and try to acquire two bottles of each malt: one to enjoy by the glass, and another to cherish as part of the collection. The usual collector's criteria apply, with the condition of the bottle label and original carton affecting desirability and value.

Locating elusive bottles can be difficult, not to mention expensive, but professional help is available. Specialist retailers such as The Whisky Exchange can turn dreams into reality, while dedicated whisky auctions at McTear's

showrooms in Glasgow are a perfect rendez-vous for the world's most avid collectors.

Among the most coveted distilleries are Springbank, Bowmore, and The Macallan, together with distilleries no longer in production, such as Port Ellen (an Islay distillery silent since 1983). Malts in limited availability, such as Dallas Dhu, Ben Wyvis, Dunglass, Kinclaith, Glen Flagler, also have an inevitable allure.

The current world record price for a malt is £25,877.50 ($41,417.20) for a 62 year old Dalmore, achieved in 2002 at McTear's. This exceeds the previous world record of £15,000 ($24,011,37) for a 60 year old Macallan in 2001.

Another high-achiever, realizing £14,300 ($22.901.79) at auction in 2001, is a bottle of Bowmore 1890. Believed to be one of the final bottlings commemorating James and William Mutter's ownership of this Islay distillery, it was personally engraved for James Mutter.

THE DALMORE 62 YEAR OLD, WHICH CONTAINS EVEN OLDER MALTS, ESTABLISHED A NEW WORLD RECORD PRICE FOR A BOTTLE OF MALT OF £25,877.50 WHEN IT WAS AUCTIONED AT MCTEAR'S SHOWROOM IN GLASGOW IN 2002

credits

Ardbeg Distillery Limited
Isle of Islay
Argyll PA42 7EB
Scotland
t.+44 (0)1496 302244
f. +44 (0)1496 302040
www.ardbeg.com

**Bruichladdich Distillery
Company Limited**
120 St. James' Building
Linwood Road
Renfrewshire PA3 3AT
Scotland
t. +44 (0)141 842 3000
f. +44 (0)141 842 3001
laddie@bruichladdich.com
www.bruichladdich.com

Bruichladdich Distillery
Isle of Islay
Argyll PA49 7UN
Scotland

**Glenfiddich and Balvenie Distilleries
William Grant & Sons Limited**
The Glenfiddich Distillery
Dufftown
Banffshire AB55 4DH
Scotland
t. +44 (0)1340 820373
f. +44 (0)1340 822083

57 Jermyn Street
London SW1Y 6LX
England
t. +44 (0)20 7495 5570
f. +44 (0)20 7495 5520

Machrie Hotel & Golf Links
Port Ellen
Isle of Islay
Argyll PA42 7AN
Scotland
t. +44 (0)1496 302310
f. +44 (0)1496 302404
machrie@machrie.com
www.machrie.com

Morrison Bowmore Distillers Ltd
Springburn Bond
Carlisle Street
Glasgow G21 1EQ
Scotland
t. +44 (0)141 558 9011
f. +44 (0)141 558 9010
or +44 (0)141 558 9413
www.morrisonbowmore.co.uk

The Scotch Malt Whisky Society
The London Members' Room
19 Greville Street
London EC1N 8SQ
England
t. +44 (0)20 7831 4447
f. +44 (0)20 7242 8494
london@smws.com
www.smws.com

The Scotch Whisky Association
t. +44 (0)131 222 9200
www.scotch-whisky.org.uk

The Whisky Exchange
t. +44 (0)20 8606 9388
www.thewhiskyexchange.com

Picture Credits

All photography by Alan Williams
(unless otherwise stated)

*51 right, 58, 59 above left and below
right* **Francesca Yorke**

59 below left **James Merrell**

59 below left center and above right
Martin Brigdale

index

acknowledgments

The publishers would like to thank everyone at the distilleries featured (see page 62) along with peat-digger Norman Campbell and Richard Burleton of the Scotch Malt Whisky Society for their help with this book.

The author would like to thank Frank McHardy and Euan Mitchell of Springbank; David Stewart of Wm Grant & Sons; Dr Bill Lumsden; Jim Cook; Graham Eunson and Claire Meikle of Glenmorangie; Jim Beveridge of United Distillers; Nick Morgan of The Classic Malts; Jim McEwan of Bruichladdich; Jim Cryle of The Glenlivet; Colin Scott of Chivas Bros; David Robertson of The Macallan; the staff of Auchentoshan; Campbell Evans of The Scotch Whisky Association; David Grant; Sukhinder Singh of The Whisky Exchange.